Soul Wounds Beyond the Scrubs: Healing the Healer

Empowering Healthcare Workers
Through Healing, Resilience and Self-Care.

Beautiful Souls

Welcome to this unique space of healing. This sixty-day journal is designed to nurture your inner child while fostering healing within the healthcare community.

Keeping a record of your journey will help you gain a deeper appreciation for holistic care, enhance your path to healing, and enable you to make a positive difference in the lives of others you care for.

Additionally, this journal is a gentle reminder of the importance of maintaining a healthy work-life balance. It encourages you to allocate time for self-care, relaxation, and hobbies that bring you joy outside of your professional responsibilities. This balance is crucial for your well-being and enhances your ability to provide compassionate care.

Embrace this opportunity to focus on healing your inner child, embracing a brighter, more compassionate future, and nurturing a balanced daily life.

With compassion and encouragement,

Dr. Kellie Diane

Publisher Awareherness Press Publishers

Awareherness@gmail.com

ISBN: 978-1-965-702-02-4

Moments of Impact:
The Small Things Matter

Day: 1

How long have you been in healthcare? What influenced your decision to pursue this career?

Day: 2

Now that you have become a healthcare professional, how do you feel about your role?

....
....
....
....
....
....
....
....
....
....
....
....
....
....
....
....
....
....
....
....
....
....
....

Day: 3

Write about one positive experience that has significantly impacted you since you began your healthcare career.

Day: 4

List five ways this experience has changed how you view your role as a healthcare professional.

Day: 5

Write about one negative experience that has significantly impacted you since your nursing career began.

....
....
....
....
....
....
....
....
....
....
....
....
....
....
....
....
....
....
....
....
....
....

Day: 6

List five ways this experience has changed how you view your role as a healthcare worker.

....
....
....
....
....
....
....
....
....
....
....
....
....
....
....
....
....
....
....
....
....
....
....

Day: 7

As healthcare workers, our shifts can sometimes be overwhelming. Write about a specific instance when you felt overwhelmed.

Day: 8

List five coping mechanisms that you have found effective in dealing with the stress of the job.

....
....
....
....
....
....
....
....
....
....
....
....
....
....
....
....
....
....
....
....
....
....
....

Day: 9

When you decided to enter healthcare, did you anticipate the current circumstances? If not, elaborate on the reasons behind your expectations.

Day: 10

How has your view of the world changed as a healthcare provider?

Day: 10

Are you feeling supported in your healthcare profession? If yes, what makes you feel supported and why?"

Reflections in the Quiet:
End-of-shift thoughts

Day: 12

What are your thoughts about your shift today? Do you feel like you made a difference? Discuss how you made a difference.

Day: 13

What methods do you use to unwind from work during your commute home? Have they been effective?

Day: 14

How do you should say feel about taking sick days? Do you ever feel guilty, as if you are letting your co-workers down? Explain how and why you think that way.

....
....
....
....
....
....
....
....
....
....
....
....
....
....
....
....
....
....
....
....
....
....
....

Day: 15

What does it feel like to show up for others consistently? Is there someone in your life who supports you as much as you help others?

Day: 16

Describe how you felt the first time you experienced loss as a healthcare provider. Were there feelings of failure, grief, or sadness?

....
....
....
....
....
....
....
....
....
....
....
....
....
....
....
....
....
....
....
....
....
....

Day: 17

"How were you able to manage and process those emotions?"

....
....
....
....
....
....
....
....
....
....
....
....
....
....
....
....
....
....
....
....
....
....
....

Day: 18

Outside of your job, who is your "go-to" person when you need to vent? Are they providing a safe place to heal? Do you have a therapist/ spiritual advisor to help you deal with these emotions?

As healthcare providers, we spend a significant amount of time each day with our colleagues, often up to 8-16 hours. How do you feel about your coworkers?.

....
....
....
....
....
....
....
....
....
....
....
....
....
....
....
....
....
....
....
....

Day: 20

How do you manage the emotional challenges of leaving your family for long hours daily? What feelings arise from balancing work responsibilities with nurturing your connection with your loved ones?

....
....
....
....
....
....
....
....
....
....
....
....
....
....
....
....
....
....
....
....
....
....
....

Day: 21

How do you cope with guilt, stress, and the determination to provide for your family? Any strategies for finding a balance between work and family life? List them below.

....
....
....
....
....
....
....
....
....
....
....
....
....
....
....
....
....
....
....
....
....

Day: 22

Do your friends and close family members acknowledge and support you professionally?

....
....
....
....
....
....
....
....
....
....
....
....
....
....
....
....
....
....
....
....
....
....

Reflection on Resilience.
Strength in Vulnerability.

Day: 23

What biases or preconceived notions may you bring to your patient interactions?

Day: 24

How did you respond to criticism feedback from your peers, patients, or supervisors?

....
....
....
....
....
....
....
....
....
....
....
....
....
....
....
....
....
....
....
....
....
....

Day: 25

Discuss your biggest fears or insecurities about your role as a Healthcare provider. How do those fears and insecurities impact your performance?

Day: 26

How do you feel about your work-life balance concerning using your PTO days??

....
....
....
....
....
....
....
....
....
....
....
....
....
....
....
....
....
....
....
....
....
....

Day: 27

Do you believe you have successfully maintained healthy boundaries with your patients? Do you become overly involved?

Day: 28

Have you incorporated any employee assistance services to assist you while on the job? Have you found it effective? Has it helped your job performance?

Day: 29

How can you support your co-workers better?

....
....
....
....
....
....
....
....
....
....
....
....
....
....
....
....
....
....
....
....
....

Day: 30

Are you secure enough to seek support from your coworkers, or are you overly independent? What wound do you believe this stems from?

....
....
....
....
....
....
....
....
....
....
....
....
....
....
....
....
....
....
....
....
....

How do you feel when your boss asks you to work overtime, and you have prior commitments? Have you set healthy boundaries for yourself, such as saying No? Do you feel guilty?

....
....
....
....
....
....
....
....
....
....
....
....
....
....
....
....
....
....
....
....
....
....
....
....

Day: 32

How was your experience working through the COVID-19 pandemic? Do you still feel like a hero, or do you believe your role is diminished through the eyes of others?

....
....
....
....
....
....
....
....
....
....
....
....
....
....
....
....
....
....
....
....
....

Have you ever had to care for a loved one, friend, or colleague on your job? How was the experience as the provider?

....
....
....
....
....
....
....
....
....
....
....
....
....
....
....
....
....
....
....
....
....

Day: 34

Have you ever lost a loved one, friend, or colleague on your job who was a patient? How was the experience as the provider?

....
....
....
....
....
....
....
....
....
....
....
....
....
....
....
....
....
....
....
....
....
....
....

Day: 35

Is there something you wish you could have said to a past patient or family member to assist them through this process? Write what you could have said or done.

....
....
....
....
....
....
....
....
....
....
....
....
....
....
....
....
....
....
....
....
....
....
....

Day: 36

How did you feel during your first code Blue? Write about your experience.

Healing and Growth
in Healthcare

Day: 37

How do you define healing in healthcare?

_____
_____
_____
_____
_____
_____
_____
_____
_____
_____
_____
_____
_____
_____
_____
_____
_____
_____
_____
_____
_____
_____
_____

Assessing your current self-care practices, how can you change them to help support your patients?

....
....
....
....
....
....
....
....
....
....
....
....
....
....
....
....
....
....
....
....
....
....
....
....

Day: 39

How do you respond to your patients and family members' emotional needs?

....
....
....
....
....
....
....
....
....
....
....
....
....
....
....
....
....
....
....
....
....

Day: 40

How can you foster a healing environment for your patients and you?

....
....
....
....
....
....
....
....
....
....
....
....
....
....
....
....
....
....
....
....
....
....

What legacy would you like to leave behind for future generations?

....

....

....

....

....

....

....

....

....

....

....

....

....

....

....

....

....

....

....

....

....

....

....

Day: 42

What five goals would you like to set for your personal and professional growth as you advance in your career?

....
....
....
....
....
....
....
....
....
....
....
....
....
....
....
....
....
....
....
....
....
....
....

Day: 43

How would you like to see the healthcare field change? What are your plans for making the changes?

....
....
....
....
....
....
....
....
....
....
....
....
....
....
....
....
....
....
....
....
....
....

Day: 44

What advice would you give to a new oncoming Healthcare worker?

Day: 45

Reflect on your feelings when faced with complex cases or patient losses. How do you handle your emotional responses to patient suffering?

....
....
....
....
....
....
....
....
....
....
....
....
....
....
....
....
....
....
....
....
....
....
....
....
....

Day: 46

How have you been able to embrace a patient's or family member's feedback to improve their healing experience?

....
....
....
....
....
....
....
....
....
....
....
....
....
....
....
....
....
....
....
....
....
....

SELF CARE

Recognizing the significance of attaining a more positive work-life balance, discuss five strategies you have in mind to make this a reality

----

Day: 48

List 5 activities that bring you joy outside of work. How many have you experienced today?

Write a letter of encouragement to yourself.

Day: 50

Create an action plan for self-love and healing. Write below what the plans will be.

....
....
....
....
....
....
....
....
....
....
....
....
....
....
....
....
....
....
....
....

Day: 51

List five things you have done to celebrate and acknowledge your contribution to healthcare.

Day: 52

Write five things that you are grateful for today.

Plan a night away from your family responsibilities if possible. What are the details?

....
....
....
....
....
....
....
....
....
....
....
....
....
....
....
....
....
....
....

Day: 54

Write a positive affirmation to yourself.

Day: 55

Write five things that you are grateful for today

....
....
....
....
....
....
....
....
....
....
....
....
....
....
....
....
....
....
....
....
....
....
....
....

Soul Wounds in Healthcare

Day: 56

Have you experienced abandonment wounds in your childhood? In what ways do you believe that it can significantly impact your job performance and interaction?

Day: 57

Have you experienced wounds in your childhood? In what ways do you believe that it can significantly impact your job performance and interaction?

....
....
....
....
....
....
....
....
....
....
....
....
....
....
....
....
....
....
....

Have you experienced wounds in your childhood? In what ways do you believe that it can significantly impact your job performance and interaction?

Day: 59

Have you experienced wounds in your childhood? In what ways do you believe that it can significantly impact your job performance and interaction?

Day: 60

Have you experienced wounds in your childhood? In what ways do you believe that it can significantly impact your job performance and interaction?

....

....

....

....

....

....

....

....

....

....

....

....

....

....

....

....

....

....

....

....

....

....

Dearest Healthcare Healer,

Congratulations on reaching the end of this 60-day journey. You have taken courageous steps toward healing, self-discovery, and transformation by engaging with these pages.

Remember, this is not merely an ending but a beautiful beginning—an opportunity to integrate the insights and lessons you've uncovered into your daily life.

Embrace the growth you've experienced and carry it with you as you navigate the world.

Know that healing is an ongoing process, and it's okay to revisit these reflections whenever you need guidance or encouragement. You are more robust and wiser than you may realize, and your journey continues to unfold in wondrous ways.

May you walk forward with an open heart, trusting in your ability to create a life filled with love, joy, and purpose. The light within you is a powerful force—share it with the world, and let it guide you toward your dreams.

With love and encouragement,

Dr Kellie Diane